W9-DET-711

Tee Ball

by Wil Mara

Content Consultant
Thomas Sawyer, EdD
Professor of Recreation and Sports Management
Indiana State University
Terre Haute, Indiana

Reading Consultant
Jeanne Clidas
Reading Specialist

Children's Press®
An Imprint of Scholastic Inc.
New York   Toronto   London   Auckland   Sydney
Mexico City   New Delhi   Hong Kong
Danbury, Connecticut

Library of Congress Cataloging-in-Publication Data
Mara, Wil.
  Tee Ball/by Wil Mara.
    p. cm.—(Rookie read about sports)
  Includes bibliographical references and index.
  ISBN-13: 978-0-531-20857-1 (lib. bdg.)   ISBN-10: 0-531-20857-5 (lib. bdg.)
  ISBN-13: 978-0-531-20926-4 (pbk.)   ISBN-10: 0-531-20926-1 (pbk.)
  1. Tee-ball—Juvenile literature. I. Title. II. Series.
  GV881.5.M33 2012
  796.357'8—dc23   2011030956

1 2 3 4 5 6 7 8 9 10 R 21 20 19 18 17 16 15 14 13 12

Photographs © 2012: Alamy Images: 14 main, 28 main (Erik Isakson/Rubberball),
cover (Jim Corwin); iStockphoto: 8, 31 bottom right (Laura Galloway), 16
(RonTech2000); Media Bakery: 6, 12 main, 18, 26, 31 top left; PhotoEdit/David
Young-Wolff: 10, 20; Shutterstock, Inc.: 4 left, 31 top right (Fotoline), 4 top right,
22, 31 bottom left (kanate), baseball throughout (Ljupco Smokovski), 24
(Sascha Burkard), 2, 4 bottom right (Svetlana Larina).

Table of Contents

What Is Tee Ball?

Tee ball is like baseball.
There are two teams.

The teams play on a field. The tee ball field has four bases. One team is in the field.

8

The other team has to hit the ball with a bat.

How to Play

The ball is on a tee. A batter hits the ball. Then he runs to first base.

A player on the other team gets the ball. Then he throws it to first base.

Another player is at first base.
He has to catch the ball.

The batter is out if the ball gets there first. She has to get off the field. Teams change sides when the batting team has three outs.

18

Getting a Run

The batter is safe if she gets there first. She stays on first base.

He goes to the next base if his team gets another hit.

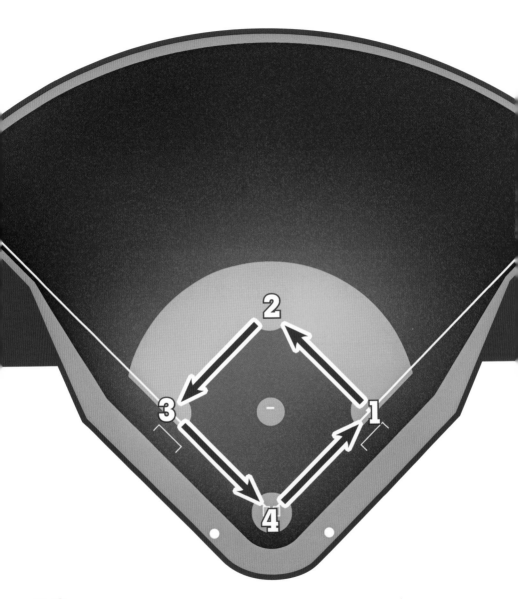

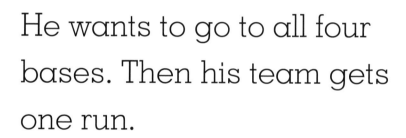

He wants to go to all four bases. Then his team gets one run.

HOME	INNING	GUESTS
3	4	2

BALL	1	STRIKE	2	OUT	2

24

Which Team Wins?

An inning is over when
both teams get three outs.
Most tee ball games have
four innings.

The team that gets the most runs wins. It does not matter if you win or lose. Tee ball is fun!

Good Sportsmanship

- Respect yourself, the other players, and the adults helping out.
- Always play fair.
- Stay positive. Cheer for your teammates. Learn from your mistakes. And keep playing!
- Be nice to all the players, whether you win or lose.

Staying Fit

Eat right.

- Choose lots of fruits and vegetables.
- Eat 5 servings of grains. Whole wheat bread is good. So is oatmeal.
- Protein keeps you strong. Meat, eggs, and fish give you protein.
- Dairy makes strong bones. Milk and cheese are dairy.

Get plenty of sleep.

Play your sport as much as you can. Tee ball players need to be strong to hit the ball with the bat. They need to be strong to throw the ball. And they need to be fast to run to the bases.

Tee Ball Fun Facts

- Tee ball games are sometimes played on the White House lawn.

- Many professional baseball players played tee ball as kids.

Visit this Scholastic web site for more information on tee ball:
www.factsfornow.scholastic.com

Words You Know

base

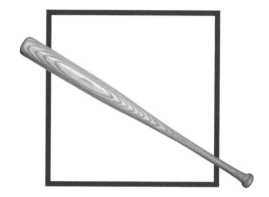

bat

field

tee

Index

About the Author

Wil Mara is the award-winning author of more than 100 books, many of them educational titles for young readers. More information about his work can be found at *www.wilmara.com*.